ARTHUR AND CONSTANCE:

OR,

THE POWER OF LOVE.

BY J. F. D. CORNELL.

* * * Ὡρμᾶτ' ἐκ θαλάμοιο, τέρεν κατὰ δάκρυ χέουσα.

NEW YORK:

WILEY & HALSTED, 351 BROADWAY.

1858.

PHAIR & CO., PRINTERS,
22 BEEKMAN STREET, NEW YORK.

ARTHUR AND CONSTANCE;

OR,

THE POWER OF LOVE.

THE fire-darting king of day
  Moved stately up on high,
From glimmering clouds, pavilion fair
  Stretched on the boundless sky.

Far off the mountains in his sight
  With numerous shades shone gay
Their sable heads his brilliant beams
  Sat on, like crowns of day.

Now happy hearts are filled with praise,
  It swells from hill and vale ;
And nature's sounds of tuneful joy
  Salute the morning, hail !

Now golden rays the castle gild
 Whose proud height, rock-built, towers;
But smiles yon humble cottage too,
 While there 'mong bright blue flowers

Two cherubs sport; so childhood sports,
 Shut out from all that's ill,
With only scenes of purest joy
 His little world to fill.

O! oft the cherub's dreamy eye
 Which looks those thoughts of love,
His curled locks and winsome ways
 Remind of those above.

With soft, delaying hand, the boy
 Her fairer hand slow drew,
While the little maid came gently on
 Amid the sparkling dew.

O! life than this is sweeter ne'er!
 When the dreamer Hope is young,
And the trying evils yet to be,
 Are never truly sung.

But little Constance' outlawed sire,
  Say, will he never come?
The cold tomb's naked marble walls,
  Make all her mother's home.

O! fatal hour of bannered might!
  Those dark brows happy are
Who wear thy changeless battle frown;
  Constance, her sire's not there.

See, where the lurid desert wide
  Looks deaths of burning thirst!
That one, does Constance call him sire,
  Who wanders here accurst?

See, where Siberia, heartless wild!
  To beasts denies to live,
Here, 'neath the cold north lights, does he
  The hope of life outlive!

The good-souled shepherd sire is kind,
  But the hermit is not he,
Ah! who folds in his arms and gazes long
  On her bright, her dark, dark eye.

The time of weeping now is past ;
  All grief is hushed to rest ;
Now Constance culls the fragrant flowers,
  A simple shepherd's guest.

His boy with Constance wiles the hours,
  Fair, fleeting, swift their speed,
Like shades of clouds in rapid flight
  Over the sunny mead.

Yet still alone for them the song
  Of wild bird carolled clear,
Or pert, upon them unawares,
  The squirrel chattered near.

Oft stood they hand in hand entranced,
  While they feasted on the view
With eye fixed on the mount's proud front,
  Serene amid the blue.

Anon, beneath the hoar sad shade
  Of burial trees they roam,
To visit cave, near sacred fane—
  The peaceful hermit's home.

The third line from the bottom of the fifth page should read thus:

But not like the hermit is he—

That airy sky of clear calm blue,
  It cannot long survive ;
Upon the mountains' ridgy tops
  The frequent tempests drive.

Whose gloomy brows of blackest night
  Look arrowy lightnings fell,
So battle rides the pleasant fields,
  With cruel eyes of hell.

When louder roll the rattling peals,
  Then closer draw the pair,
More lovely far thus hastening on
  Beneath the lightning's glare.

Or if long-shadowed sunset sank
  Unnoted into night,
Though far from home, was Arthur there,
  To Constance all was light.

Oft o'er the story of a ghost
  They both in terror shook,
While their tiny barks unheeded danced
  Far down the fretful brook.

Round guileless hearts thus, day by day,
Were twined love's golden bands,
Themselves unconscious of the links
Thus bound by angel hands.

All goodly graces gild young love
When beauty reigns supreme !
The warmest, gentlest, softest flame,
Is when young lovers dream.

Now noiseless time that changes all
Wakes Constance every charm ;
Beside the manly Arthur sits,
In true love-silence calm.

Right cheerly blaze the curling flames
In many a curious form,
Hark ! loudly wails the surly blast—
Old Winter rides the storm.

Both eyes are resting on that flame,
Both bent heads muse the day
Of heart-lived childhood's shadowy joys,
That knew nor feared decay.

When hand in hand, and cheek to cheek,
  O'er the same page they bent,
One kerchief dried each mingled tear,
  Each sigh both bosoms sent.

E'en now, unconscious to themselves,
  The sigh unbidden falls,
While memory lifts her fairy veil,
  And all the past recals.

Why rove to other days, when youth,
  Joy-browed, seeks not the past?
Days of my youth rise to my view!
  Would such days were my last!

Home of my childhood! when I leave
  Thy memory-sainted bowers,
Will not regretful murmurs sigh
  For childhood's rosy hours?

'Tis this that makes the young thoughts steal
  Up from their silent home,
And rouses up the sleeping tears,
  Those tears that still will come.

He takes her little hand in his,
  Reads all the melting eye,
Then heart to heart, in transport wild,
  Rush, heave, throb silently.

Now lip to lip, now lip on neck,
  No word can sorrow find,
Grief-drooping lids the while rain tears,
  That leave all words behind.

Yet ere he leaves his gentle heart,
  To seek a distant shore,
He traced these lines upon her book—
  One last embrace, 'tis o'er.

The tolling bell with rising knell,
  Tells of loved one far away,
His bosom burns as mourner turns,
  Sighing for friend that's far away.

Bell-like, my love, this line may prove
  To reader's heart for one away,
Bosom may burn, as sad she'll turn
  To words, the sighs of friend away.

Like mourner's tear, that falls o'er bier
  Of loved one gone to rest away,
Her pearly tear 'll fall gently here,
  And dew the sighs of friend away.

Now proudly swells the snowy sail
  Above the crested wave,
And nobly rides the gallant bark
  That bears the good and brave.

Old England's loved and merry world,
  Now trembles on the sight,
Fair as the golden king's last beam
  Just sinking into night.

'Tis gone, a soldier must not grieve,
  Thy griefs and cares disband,
Hark! martial music, wildly sweet,
  Rolls backward to the strand.

Now haste we o'er the slow sad years
  That sweep their gloomy train,
Now haste we to the happy hour
  When lovers meet again.

Stay not to count the thousand hopes,
  And dreams, and fears, and prayers,
The happy hour seems on the wing
  That shall redeem their cares.

E'en now the warrior's straining eye
  Peers anxious o'er the sea,
His look is toward his longed-for home—
  Old England, 'tis for thee!

Now wind's and tide's and battle's roar
  Are hushed, a single note,
The solitary wood bird's lay
  Renews the past remote.

Painted within his breaking heart
  That home was still the same:
The tree, the vine, the cot were there,
  But ah! no Constance came.

This steals away the light from heaven;
  Rifles the floweret's bloom,
This stills the sweetest songster's note,
  This hangs each tree in gloom.

Can sable garb or priestly robe
  Or steel the heart from woe?
Can gloom of mossy cave efface
  A father's fond love? No!

Haste soldier! Hie thee to this cell,
  Here is a home for thee,
Meet for the one whose days must now
  With love and sorrow be.

Yet, Constance lives! the quick thoughts
      speak
  Voiceless, yet heart to heart,
The soldier writes, the hermit vows
  Her eye shall read; they part.

Her gentle form he saw within
  The castle's frowning wall;
And to his tears, as she were crazed
  She answered not his call!

As when the dark cloud folds the lightning red gleaming,
  So lover's sad brow hides the fire of love,
When that lightning has shivered the lord of the forest,
  So love rends the soul that with Constance is wove.

As when the soft rain wears away with its drippings
  Those fragments that tell the wild lightning's career,
So sorrow, slow brooding, destroys all the tokens
  Which tell the rude lightning has even been here.

A rainbow thy smile is ; but ah 'tis another's,
The serpentine lightning more pleases my sight,
Let it bury myself and my woes in oblivion,
Sorrow weeps not in the calm of death's night.

Perchance, then I'll dream that oft times in the even
There 'll come a fair form to bend over my grave,
The bow in the cloud, and the sun veiled in glory,
No storm, no lightning, no tempest to brave.

But softly as melt the fair colors of Iris,
Their beauties will seem to unite in my love,
As the rainbow which erst bent all lovely in heaven,
She'll bend o'er my grave, as the rainbow above.

And the stars one by one shall look down in their pity,
And Cynthia's beam shall fall lightly and pale,
And the bird of the even shall pour forth its sorrow,
The winds and the far distant waters shall wail.

My spirit shall drink in the sighs that are breaking,
Shall treasure unseen the blue tear of her eye,
Shall fold round the bosom that heaves in its sorrow,
With Constance return to its home in the sky.

Now ills and sorrows lightly press,
His slumbers ne'er they'll break,
No sound is there save the light hum
The wavy branches make.

She read whom stony walls confined,
  And all her heart springs wept;
And all her love ran out to meet—
  The cold bars intercept.

Can walls of stone and iron bars
  Repress love's gentle flame?
Are these the arms that lovers use
  To win the Cyprian dame?

So thinks this lord of many a mead
  And many a wavy wood,
Whose proud possessions cross the mount
  And many a running flood.

Can the bold eagle love his cage,
  The dove forget her mate?
Nor love they, nor forget they e'er,
  'Till death—the lover's fate.

Soon calm the eagle's black wings fold,
  The dove, soft nestling, dies,
His fiery eye, her tender gaze.
  All change of love defies.

Now fling aside the bars and bolts,
Back roll each massy door,
Now surely love will come and bide—
The rival is no more.

See how yon golden sun descends
Fast from the realms of light,
Like some good man's last gaze which
beams
Most beauteous in death's night.

'Tis eve—behold a haughty form
Within a lonely room,
One hears—"Thy soldier's dead, this night
Thine eye shall read his tomb!"

That sun doled forth her grief's last day,
His latest ray has fled,
Now may she read the dismal stone
Which speaks her soldier dead.

'Twas near the time of falling leaves.
When summer sweetly dies—
She folds herself in softest shades,
And melts away in sighs.

Her vesture was the faintest hue
  That decks the dying flower,
Her breath was roses perishing
  In every wild wood bower.

Above, night's thousand golden lights,
  Soft beaming, did illume,
The hornéd moon in gentle rays
  Stole through the forest gloom.

A lone hoar chapel guards the wood
  Where the ivy nods in gloom
And the statues mourn in marble pride
  O'er many a grassy tomb.

At the gleam of morn, at the dusk of eve,
  Here a holy hermit strays,
His thoughts are fixed on better things,
  He lives in prayer and praise.

How calmly lives whose hopes whose joys
  Are all beyond the tomb,
How happy hastes that parting soul
  Which fears no final doom.

The silent airs stealing among
  These arches green of pine,
Remind of better, earlier hours—
  Sweet hours that once were mine.

Hours when with heart untaught to scan
  The treacherous ways of men,
Methought as true as beautiful
  The world. 'Tis changed from then.

But fairer than each form of stone,
  And softer than each stilly air,
Yet like the trembling ivy sad,
  Stands pale, pure, lovely Constance there.

See through her beauteous locks how shines
  That face of peerless light,
So heaven's pure diamond eyes look down
  To cheer the moonless night.

Oh not the limner's curious shade
  Can paint the good and fair,
That pale brow marks the spirit good
  Which sits enthronéd there.

Plays round that beauty-arching mouth,
Beams from that pensive eye
That tells a world of love now dead,
And Constance, too, must die!

She stood the moonlight graves among,
'Neath the old arching wood,
As angel watchers stand to guard
The last sleep of the good.

But hark! how swells the midnight air
With heavy-tolling bell,
Hark! poor heart breaking at the sound!
She drooped as it solemnly fell.

She starts, she sighs, with her small hands
raised
To the still heaven she uttered a prayer
Amid the dismal deathy shades
Why strays an angel there?

Why trickles down a silent tear
At every tolling bell?
Why mock the winds a grief so fair
In the lone forest dell?

Sad sisters! solitude and grief
Yours are full many a sigh
And many a tear, too good to meet
The world's cold tearless eye.

Then angels from the better world
Descend on wings of love,
And treasure up your crystal tears,
And bear your sighs above.

The same old haunts of playful hours
In every hedge she sees,
The same old solemn whispers ring
Round yellow autumn's trees.

Softly and sad the hermit sleeps
In yon rude cheerless cell,
These rain-worn stones she often read,
But wild the letters spell.

Young Arthur starts from every hedge,
His name the still airs call,
Each time-worn letter starting out
Writes Arthur over all.

Still strays the last, long, echoing knell
  Upon the waiting ear.
That vainly lists the dying sound
  Repeated still to hear.

'Twas then as though her task were o'er,
  She sank on the dewy bed,
Where the long grass waved dreamily
  Above the sleeper's head.

Again the deep-mouthed curfew tolled,
  Nor sigh, nor tear, nor groan,
How placid sweet a face death bowed
  Upon that marble stone.

Grim death-bell toll not, she is gone,
  Dead are all Constance' woes—
A land of pure love greets the eye
  Which death thus sweetly closed.

The thoughtless winds her raven locks
  Float careless streaming by,
While the moonbeam'sshadow-flitting light
  Looks on in revery.

The naked boughs their thin shade wave
Across that face how slow,
Where the long, still, silken lashes rest
Upon a seam of snow.

In vain death's iron seal may press,
To crush each beauteous trace,
Still may you read an imaged heaven
Upon that silent face.

'Tis Arthur's lines, the last he traced
Who lies beneath her feet,
Still clasps them yet that thin white hand,
Though life has ceased to beat.

Only the noiseless rabbit came,
Gazed up in her still fair face,
Crept to the small foot that moves no more
A leaf stirred he fled the place.

The night-blue heaven looks cold and pure,
The golden stars look peace,—
That heaven bends down o'er lover dead—
Stars whisper happiness!

It is a life that angels lead
  In a land of endless love,
The soul's pure feelings are the breath
  The angels breathe above.

Next eve the mossy mantling sod
  Closed lightly o'er a pair,
The hermit sire and Constance lay
  With gentle Arthur there.

That outcast sire, his lot no more
  The cavern drear and wild—
Sweet realm of bliss return him all,
  A home, his wife, his child.

I love to linger when the sun
  Dies in the golden west,
Among the solemn silent dead,
  To think upon the blest.

I love the yellow rustling leaf,
  And autumn's gentlest breath,
For then I think that heaven is hid
  Beneath the garb of death.

The spirit then recals its loves,
When round us beauty dies,
For dying beauty leads the mind
To beauty's home—the skies.

Hast ever seen a lovely tomb?
Hast ever heard dead love?
Hast ever felt the holy thrill
The grave brings from above?

Then come with me to yonder tomb
Sad with the willow's shade,
There thou shalt see, hear, feel dead love,
For there is Constance laid.

Bring cypress—here the good is laid,
Here sleep the wise and fair;
Let death-flowers, white and beautiful,
Float on this mournful air.

Bring cypress, cypress! What so soon
Has the young life fled away?
This is love's power,—it palls with night,
Sweet morn's most brilliant ray!

www.ingramcontent.com/pod-product-compliance
Lightning Source LLC
LaVergne TN
LVHW011140110826
845150LV00008B/2438

* 9 7 8 1 4 1 8 1 9 2 6 1 7 *